I0504442

Advertising Concept

and Copywriting

Using the

Unique Selling Proposition

Mike Swedenberg

Copyright © 2016 James Michael Swedenberg

All rights reserved.

No part of this work covered by the copyright hereon may be reproduced or

used in any form or by any means, graphic, electronic or mechanical, including

photocopying, recording, taping, Web distribution or information storage retrieval

systems without the written permission of:

James Michael Swedenberg.

TRADEMARK INFORMATION

All trademarks, trade names and logos mentioned or used in this

publication are the property of their respective owners.

Cover Design and Photograph by

Mike Swedenberg

For permission to use material from this product, submit your request to

mike@swedenberg.com

ISBN-13: 978-1511604741

ISBN-10 1511604743

DEDICATION

To my Copywriting instructors at the School of Visual Arts back in the 1970s. Jay Michael Wolf and Ken Charof. You explained the Unique Selling Proposition well enough so even I could understand. Your class, "How to Write an Ad and How to make it Better" influenced my creative and sales career in ways you could never imagine

MOST GOOD COPYWRITERS

are very strange people who have only reached copywriting after eliminating
every other means of making a living through writing. Once a man becomes
resigned to making a good living by writing a few words at a time and
writing them over and over again in various combinations, he is likely to
think of himself as a professional copywriter.

Howard Gossage

CONTENTS

Early Copywriting

Very good ground Coffee
for *EightShillings* a Pound, 14 Ounces to the Pound'
which is the Extent of what it makes when properly,
roafted, to be Sold by *Ifrael Eaton*, living near the
Mill-Bridge ;——where Perfons may have Chocolat ;
and alfo Coffee ground for *Eighteen Pence* a Pound.

[1]

And the Critics

"Whatever is common is despised. Advertisements are now so numerous
that they are very negligently perused, and it is therefore become necessary
to gain attention by magnificence of promises, and by eloquence sometimes
sublime and sometimes pathetick."
Samuel Johnson: Idler #40 (January 20, 1759)

---

[1] Very Good Ground Coffee for Eight Shillings a Pound." Boston, May 1761.

Contemporary Copywriting

Fresh Roasted Coffee is completely committed to providing our customers
with the highest quality coffee on earth.

The Fresh Roasted Coffee process begins at the source. Our coffees are
chosen and established with great love and greater yet - consideration of
origin, flavor profile and quality. All of these components help us to deliver
consistent, exceptional coffee with true approachability. Fresh Roasted
Coffee roasts our beans using the most eco-friendly roasting technology
available. We have eliminated our carbon emissions by up to 80 percent in a
smokeless roasting environment which increases overall flavor and quality.
Freshness is the key to revealing all of what coffee has to offer. Our beans
are roasted per order and shipped directly to your door. We want our
customers to experience coffee at its peak drinkability just a few days after
being roasted to perfection. Our process reaches completion when you
truly taste a coffee's origin...and nothing extra.[2]

And the Critics:

"There are ads in schools, airport lounges, doctors' offices, movie theaters,
hospitals, gas stations, elevators, convenience stores, on the Internet, on
fruit, on ATMs, on garbage cans and countless other places. There are ads
on beach sand and restroom walls." [3]

"One of the ironies of advertising in our times is that as commercialism
increases, it makes it that much more difficult for any particular advertiser
to succeed, hence pushing the advertiser to even greater efforts."[4]

---

[2] Fresh Roasted Coffee LLC
[3] "Ad Creep — Commercial Alert". Commercialalert.org.
[4] McChesney, Robert W. "The Political Economy of Media: Enduring Issues, Emerging Dilemmas". Monthly Review Press, New York, (May 1, 2008), p. 266

Mike Swedenberg

What is Copywriting

"If you can't explain it simply, you don't understand it well enough."
Albert Einstein

Copywriters, sometimes referred to as a creative content provider, is a professional skilled in the art of writing words for advertising, sales and marketing. It includes the Concept, Headline, Body Copy and sometimes the Visual Image. Said another way, it is the words in an ad that explains the product or service.

Copywriting is used to promote an idea, product, person, business or opinion. The reader of the ad should be motivated to purchase the product or called to action as in political ads that sway voters to cast a ballot for a particular candidate.

The craft is protected by the First Amendment and thus there is no license required to be a copywriter, but you have to study to be one to achieve any success.

I received my basic training at The School of Visual Arts in Manhattan and my advanced degree on the front lines in a dozen or so New York agencies. This coupled with Persuasive Selling training at Procter & Gamble has benefited my career in many ways. I hope to share that knowledge with you.

1

Duties of a Copywriter

"Early to bed, early to rise. Work like hell and advertise."
Ted Turner

Develop concepts for advertising

Write headlines

Write the content of the body copy

Create taglines

Write catalogues, brochures and sales material.

Content for Television and radio advertising

Sales letters

Press releases

White papers

Billboards and other outdoor advertising

Webpage text and other Internet content

Write email campaigns

Social media

Search Engine Optimization (SEO)

Keywords and Meta tags

Mobile advertising and Apps

The last six duties did not exist when I began my career. In

1972, a Copywriting instructor told our class that everything that can possible be done in advertising and marketing has already been created. You have print, outdoor, television and radio. That's it; there are no other avenues. He said this about 20 years before the Internet and Digital media was available to the general public. Who knew? Not me; otherwise I would have bought Yahoo, AOL, Apple and Microsoft stock at their IPOs and I'd be living in Tahiti phoning in this book to a ghostwriter.

You will have these duties and stuff that hasn't been thought of yet but will one day be dropped on your desk for you to write as if you're the expert.

"Hey, Joe. Our client just invented a Double Barreled Atomic Sotinator. I have no idea what it is, but give us 600 words of copy by 5 p.m. None of that generic stuff either. Make the copy snappy."

How the craft has changed over the years.

"The right name is an advertisement in itself." - Claude C. Hopkins

Kelly Robbins, Founder of The Copywriting Institute, recently wrote "The importance of the role copywriting plays in advertising has expanded exponentially in the last 150 years. In 1866 Claude Hopkins, one of the founding fathers of copywriting, was revolutionary in his idea to research consumers before writing copy and to do test marketing before launching a widespread campaign. Today, the Internet revolution has brought ever-changing business Web sites, inexpensive e-zines, search engine optimization (SEO), blogging and social networking sites, such as MySpace, Twitter and Facebook, all of which are rapidly changing the way the world communicates." [5]

When I started in the business, Mobile Advertising meant ads displayed on mobile vehicles like buses, taxicabs and subway trains. Now it's advertising on Smart Phones and iPads providing customers with personalized information for goods, services and ideas.

The web was something a spider wove to catch flies. Now it's something companies use to catch customers.

A tablet was a piece of slate used to scribe the 10 commandments. Now it's a vehicle for mobile advertising and reading books.

---

[5] The Copywriting Evolution by Kelly Robbins Are your copywriting skills keeping up with society?

Where Copywriters work

"Copy is a direct conversation with the consumer." Shirley Polykoff

Ad Agencies

Retail, Mail-order houses and online stores

Newspapers

Manufacturers

Media including TV, Radio and Web

Banks

Insurance

Financial institutions

Non-profits

Education

Healthcare

Political Parties

Sports

Entertainment

And of course Freelancers who work undependably for any of the categories listed above.

List of Famous Copywriters

"Simplicity is the ultimate sophistication." – Leonardo Da Vinci

This is a list of well-known advertising copywriters who founded a major multinational agency, have been inducted into an advertising hall of fame, have been recognized with a lifetime achievement award, or have considerable influence in the copywriting world.

David Abbott, founder of Abbott Mead Vickers BBDO

William Bernbach, founder of DDB Worldwide

Drayton Bird, founder of THB&W

Leo Burnett, founder of Leo Burnett Worldwide

Fairfax M. Cone, founder of Foote Cone & Belding

Bernice Fitz-Gibbon, 1982 Advertising Hall of Fame inductee

Jo Foxworth, key writer at McCann Erickson

Stan Freberg

David Ogilvy, founder of Ogilvy & Mather

Dave Trott Founder of GGT, Bainsfair Sharkey Trott and former Chairman and Executive Creative Director of The Gate London, copywriter, blogger and author

Former copywriters:

Many creative people spend time early in their careers working as advertising copywriters. This is a list of those who worked as copywriters before achieving fame in a non-advertising career. The names are followed by the careers in which they are famous.

Sherwood Anderson, author

Augusten Burroughs, author

Helen Gurley Brown, former publisher and editor (Cosmopolitan)

Peter Carey, author

Bryce Courtenay, author

Don DeLillo, author

Kenny Everett, comedian and radio DJ

F. Scott Fitzgerald, author

Terry Gilliam, director and animator

Alec Guinness, actor

Dashiell Hammett, author

Hugh Hefner, publisher (Playboy)

Joseph Heller, author

Russell Hoban, author

John Hughes, director, writer

Thom Jones, author

Tim Kazurinsky, comedian

Elmore Leonard, author

Rick Moranis, actor

Ogden Nash, poet

Bob Newhart, comedian and actor

Alan Parker, director

Steven Pressfield, author

Franc Roddam, director

Salman Rushdie, author

John Safran, documentarian and broadcaster

Indra Sinha, author

Dorothy L. Sayers, author

Chrissie Swan, TV and radio presenter

Fay Weldon, author [6]

---

[6] Source: Wikipedia April 1, 2015

The Link Between Copywriting
and Direct Sales

The longest word in the English language is the one following
"And now, a word from our sponsor."
Hal Eaton

Direct sales is when a salesperson sells you his or her product or service face to face. Advertising is a close cousin to direct selling. An agency employs many of the same principles as a direct sales rep to motivate a consumer to buy something.

I bring to the table not only a decade in advertising but three decades of direct sales for Fortune 50 Companies.

You may think of sales as an entirely different industry from advertising. Actually, they're closely related. Selling by way of a newspaper, radio, TV, Mobile or Internet ad, is the most difficult type of sale.

In direct sales a salesperson can probe, uncover objections and close a sale on the spot. In advertising all you can do is suggest that the customer take action as in, "Visit our showroom and test drive our new Whizmobile."

There is no guarantee that the people you are reaching are in the market to buy a car or if they would be interested in your particular brand if they were shopping around. The objective is to motivate those who are shopping for a particular style of car, to visit the sponsor's dealership so the salesman can close the deal.

The things a salesperson takes for granted in direct selling are lacking in advertising although that is changing with tools like Organic Advertising and Ad Remarketing.

Think of Organic Advertising as the listings on search engine results pages because of their relevance to the search terms you entered, as opposed to the paid ads that are displayed usually on the right hand side of your screen.

Drew Barton, in an article published on SouthernWeb.com, best described Ad remarketing as a "tool used by web advertisers to bring potential customers back to their websites after they've left. By keeping track of a customer's browsing habits, companies can in effect give the customer a second chance at buying their product."

This is helpful in reaching a target market but it has flaws. I have published a series of study guides for the US Immigration test in eight languages. I am constantly scouring the web for my books and those of my competitors. As a result, the ads that appear on my screen and email offers from Amazon are often for my own books and sometimes my competitors. I understand that they are there only because I did a Google search for my titles, but it is a waste of time because I am the author of the book and will not be a buyer no matter how many times I see the ads.

In direct selling a sales rep would never try to sell dental equipment to a plumber, but as an advertising copywriter you often have little control of your audience. You pay for circulation in a particular magazine, TV program, newspaper or search engine and try to target market a particular segment to expose your product to as many people as possible. You hope your potential customers will see the ad, and respond by purchasing your product. Even if you run the ad in a specialty magazine or newspaper, you still are paying for exposure to readers who aren't potential clients. It is a shotgun approach that's inefficient.

An example is disposable baby diapers. The manufacturer runs an ad on a TV program in an attempt to reach newborn mothers or expectant parents. But only a fraction of the viewers are potential customers who can be motivated to action. You're able to narrow your audience by the selection of media, newborn magazines, TV programming aimed at women of child bearing age, and the internet providers who are adept at target marketing niche markets, but you still hit people who will never buy a disposable diaper.

As a representative for a multi-national publishing company, I sold law books to attorneys in my Manhattan territory. I could target market my sales call and presentation to attorneys who practiced in a specific specialty of law, Personal Injury for example. I could adapt my presentation on the fly by asking questions I knew from experience that would interest a Personal Injury attorney. The publisher I worked for, on the other hand, spent millions a year on ads to the legal profession to gain brand recognition and maybe entice an attorney to call for a catalog or sales rep.

Even though I could only call on about 150 prospects a week, I was able to close enough business to make a great living. My publishing company could reach tens of thousands of attorneys with one trade ad but the response rate was very low.

In summary, direct sales and advertising share many of the same principles and are closely related, but the job of a copywriter is difficult.

The Unique Selling Proposition

"Every product has a unique personality and it is your job to find it."

Joe Sugarman

The Unique Selling Proposition[7] (USP) and why people who think they understand it, really don't.

I was involved in a discussion on LinkedIn focus group that was dedicated to Copywriting. We were arguing over the effectiveness of taglines and the use of a USP. One of the Copywriters said there is no such thing as a USP since no product is unique. His example was there are hundreds of makes and models of cars, nothing unique about them.

I replied, "No difference between a Mercedes and a Hyundai? There is nothing unique about a Porsche or a Volvo?" There is no fastest car, or largest SUV, or least expensive or best gas mileage? Nothing unique about a Chevy Volt or 600 horsepower Mustang GT? They are all the same?"

He still disagreed and said, they are all classified as cars. Now if there was just one car make in the world then that would be unique. The debate raged on. He's wasn't a bad guy, he just hadn't grasped

---

[7] Also known as the Unique Selling Point

the concept of a USP and he was resistant to the concept.

I studied copywriting at the School of Visual Arts in New York. I took several courses with different instructors; however, the best class was "How to Write an Ad and How to Make It Better." It focused on developing the concept of the ad more than the actual writing of copy. Most in the class failed to grasp the technique; then, one night it hit me like a bolt. From that moment on, I've used that knowledge as the foundation of my sales, marketing and advertising career.

Rosser Reeves of Ted Bates & Company, coined the term Unique Selling Proposition sometimes referred to as a positioning statement . "Find a unique aspect of the product, something no one else could say about their product, and make that the focal point of the advertisement."

In *Reality in Advertising* Reeves wrote that "The USP is widely misunderstood." He explains, "Each advertisement must make a proposition to the consumer. Not just words, not just product puffery, not just show-window advertising. Each advertisement must say to each reader, "Buy this product, and you will get this specific benefit."

"The proposition must be one that the competition either cannot, or does not, offer. It must be unique in either a feature of the brand or a claim not otherwise made in that particular field of advertising. The proposition must be so strong that it can move the mass millions, i.e., pull over new customers to your product..."[8]

Perhaps yours is the only product of its kind made in America. Perhaps a testing lab rated it as the best made in the world. It could be something as simple as the only product without some scary sounding ingredient or lower in fat content.

The only chocolate candy manufactured in a small Pennsylvania town is a USP, but it may only be significant to consumers who live in the surrounding communities who take pride in local products. It is meaningless to those living several states away and has little value to them. That being said, a candy made in Switzerland half a world

[8] In Reality in Advertising (Reeves 1961, pp. 46–48)
[9] Betty Louis Inc.® Just Great Stuff

away would be a higher perceived value because of the reputation of Swiss chocolate. Yet the two products could be equal in quality. How would you handle each?

Business author Neil Rackham believes a value proposition consists of four main parts: capability, impact, proof, and cost.[10]

Capability: What your product or service does.

Impact: What difference it will make to the consumer

Proof: What evidence do you present to support your USP.

Cost: What is the cost ratio to the benefit.

Keep in mind the balance between the benefit and value of the benefit. Will the value resonate with the consumer?

A $200,000 car may have the best gas mileage in its class, but would that value resonate with the target market? Would it be a factor for consumers shopping for cars under $10,000?

The full-on champagne cooler in the Bentley Mulsanne will have appeal to their customers but would be a joke to those shopping for a low end econobox.

---

[10] MERGE: Simplify the Complex Sale in Five Surefire Steps By William L. MacDonald AuthorHouse 2011

Actual examples of USPs:

Fleischmann's Simply Homemade Baking Mix Cornbread

AllOver Media, Largest Network, Most Coverage.

Chevrolet Camaro, Motor Trend's Car of the year for 2016.

North American Airlines has the highest overall score in the J.D. Power and Associates 2015 North America Airline Satisfaction Study.

A USP is often defined as being the fastest, shortest, longest, thinnest, bulkiest, most expensive, least expensive, number one rated, rarest, most advanced, available in the widest range, simpler, most complex, longest track record and so forth. Yes, being the worst rated is a USP, but I don't suggest you go that route. Remember the adage, accentuate the positive and deemphasize the negative.

Be specific on your claim to increase believability. Claiming your client is a large source of auto parts for the collectible car market is not specific and instantly forgettable. Saying they stock over one million parts for collectible cars from the 1960s is specific and would resonate with collectable car owners..

Document your claim with bona fide sources. Your client's silicon spray may be environmentally safe, but proving it with the Underwriter's Laboratories GREENGUARD Certification Standard for Chemical Emissions for Building Materials, Finishes and Furnishings removes any doubt about the claim.

Is your client willing to guarantee their product or service? How far are they willing to go? Hyundai is not the only manufacturer to offer a 10 year, 100,000 mile powertrain warranty but they also provides vehicle owners with a five-year, unlimited-mile 24-hour roadside-assistance service, which includes towing, battery jump-starts, flat-tire changing and lock-out assistance. As one of the best car warranties, it is good for original and subsequent owners.[11]

IMPORTANT: Saying you're the best cellphone provider or make the greatest tasting coffee is not a USP. That is a matter of opinion, not irrefutable fact. Remember, not all USPs are created equal. Some are strong some are weak.

For most products, if you read through all of the fluff in the

---

[11] 7 automakers with the best car warranties. By Margarette Burnette • Bankrate.com

body copy of previous ads, instruction manual or product insert

material, you may find the USP buried in the small print. Use that

hidden feature and benefit to promote your product.

Assignment:

Flip through a magazine or newspaper and look for generic sounding headlines. See if there is a USP buried in the copy that would make a better headline.

Actual Examples:

Car Dealer Ad Headline: Extravaganza Blowout.

Buried in the body copy: Number one in Customer Satisfaction three years in a row as measured by Auto Dealer Rater. (What do you think attracts more buyers, a low ball price or continued great customer service long after the purchase is over?)

Restaurant Ad Headline: Bring Your Appetite.

Buried in the body copy Michelin Rating Three Stars. A restaurant worth a special journey with exceptional cuisine where diners eat extremely well, often superbly. Distinctive dishes are precisely executed, using superlative ingredients.

Ringing Endorsements and the USP

"If you can't turn yourself into a consumer, you probably shouldn't be in the advertising business at all." —Leo Burnett

12

Fleischmann's® Simply Homemade Baking Mix Cornbread won a coveted ChefsBest® Award for Best Taste. They prominently displayed it on the package front. This USP made the package stand out on the grocer's shelf when displayed next to the competition.

Using a spokesperson to promote your brand is effective and is a USP since they do not endorse the completive products as well. Some are more effective than others.

When Sean "Diddy" Combs agreed to endorse Ciroc Vodka® in 2009, sales jumped from 40,000 cases annually to 2 million.[13]

The Federal Trade Commission has strict guide lines on the definition and use of endorsements and testimonials hat you must be aware of before using one. Here are a few of the examples they offer. Please see the complete guidelines as sourced below.[14]

---

[12] Fleischmann's Simply Homemade Baking Mix Cornbread

[13] Advertising Age. Celebrity Endorsements Still Push Product- DeanCrutchfield. Sept. 22, 2010.

[11] This document includes only the text of the Revised Endorsement and Testimonial Guides. To learn more, read the Federal Register Notice at www.ftc.gov/opa/2009/10/endortest.shtm.

Endorsements must reflect the honest opinions, findings, beliefs, or experience of the endorser. Furthermore, an endorsement may not convey any express or implied representation that would be deceptive if made directly by the advertiser.

Example 1: A film critic's review of a movie is excerpted in an advertisement. When so used, the review meets the definition of an endorsement because it is viewed by readers as a statement of the critic's own opinions and not those of the film producer, distributor, or exhibitor.

Example 2: A TV commercial depicts two women in a supermarket buying a laundry detergent. The women are not identified outside the context of the advertisement. One comments to the other how clean her brand makes her family's clothes, and the other then comments that she will try it because she has not been fully satisfied with her own brand. This obvious fictional dramatization (Slice of Life) of a real life situation would not be an endorsement.

Example 3: In an advertisement for a pain remedy, an announcer who is not familiar to consumers except as a spokesman for the advertising drug company praises the drug's ability to deliver fast and lasting pain relief. He purports to speak, not on the basis of his own opinions, but rather in the place of and on behalf of the drug company. The announcer's statements would not be considered an endorsement.

Example 4: A television advertisement for a particular brand of golf balls shows a prominent and well-recognized professional golfer practicing numerous drives off the tee. This would be an endorsement by the golfer even though she makes no verbal statement in the advertisement.

What is an Advertising Concept?

"You can have everything you want in life if you will help enough people get what they want." – Zig Ziglar

An advertising campaign is built around a clear, brief statement. The concept is a story comprised of two things, what is told and how it's told. Here is a great ad concept, simple and direct:

With only four words, the copywriter made Shiner beer stand out from the completion. The product still uses the original 1909 recipe and unlike others who promote their brand with the cliché "New and Improved."

This is not a USP since there are German brewers that have not changed their recipe since the 15th Century and there are American breweries who can make the same claim, but it is part of a subset.[15]

---

[15] ." Ad Agency: McGarrah Jessee 2013

In this 1992 ad, the copywriter developed a concept that the airline held its prices while others raised theirs in a attention getting way. Depending on the air fare market at the time, this may or may not be a USP since other airlines could have had held their fares as well. It is, however, a great concept and memorial headline. I could even make the case that the body copy was unnecessary. All that was needed was the headline, visual and address line for an impactful ad.

In summary, develop a concept that is unique to the product or service and build a campaign around it.

---

[16] Agency: GSD&M

Divorce yourself from your work.

"Advertising is only evil when it advertises evil things." – David Ogivly

My SVA copywriting instructors, Jay and Ken told us on day one that we need to place our personal bias and preferences aside and do our best work for all of our clients.

Let's say you are a dyed in the wool Democrat and landed the Republican candidate's campaign account. It's your professional responsibility to write damn good copy that would help the Republican win. Afterwards, you can go and vote for his opponent. They called it "divorcing yourself from your work."

They gave examples of criminal defense attorneys who took on despicable lowlife clients and fought hard to defend them and to get them off, even if they suspected their client was guilty.

A surgeon works just as hard to save the life of a wounded criminal as they do to save the life of the police officer whom the criminal had shot.

A professional journalist reports an incident without their personal opinion shading the story, while a hack would twist and distort the story to fit their personal agenda. Have you ever seen a reporter gush over one candidate and then treat his opponent with disrespect? That is all too common and unprofessional.

It is unethical for you to accept a client and then do less than your best on their advertising because you disagree with their politics or their product.

I have argued this philosophy with other creatives in the industry and I'm sad to report more disagree with me than agree. However, not one said they would take the client's money and sabotage the campaign. They would simply refuse to work on the account. A few said they would accept the work if they needed the money but their whole heart would not be in it.

An anti-smoker refuses to work on a cigarette ad even though it's a legal product. A copywriter refuses to work on a client's automobile campaign because he believes the car is a gas guzzler and harms the environment. The possibilities are endless and you can rationalize away anything.

Some say that the rules of doctors and lawyers don't apply to copywriters because we aren't professionals. I say we are in every sense pros.

Others will cite extreme examples such as: "Would you handle the Klu Klux Klan radio spots? How about the banner ads for the Child Molester Benevolent Association? Would you write the New American Nazi Party bumper sticker slogan?" Of course not, those are ridiculous examples. I'm talking about legal and moral mainstream products and services that would come across your desk every day. You should be able to do great work for Chevrolet even if you're a Ford fan, the Boston Red Sox if you're a Yankee fan, or accept a beer account even if you don't drink. A great example would be accepting work for a cheap wine maker even though you're a wine snob.

If you can't separate, or divorce yourself from your work, you need to find a new profession. You will have too many conflicts, do your clients a disservice and limit the scope of your work.

Generic Advertising

"When I write an advertisement, I don't want you to tell me that you find it 'creative.' I want you to find it so interesting that you buy the product."
David Ogilvy

The difference between Generic and Institutional Advertising is that the former is the result of bad, lazy writing that can be used by almost any company, a one size fits all. Institutional ads are well-crafted campaigns that promote a company or industry to gain awareness without promoting a particular product or service.

"Public Service Announcements (PSA) and community outreach programs are examples of institutional advertising. These types of advertising promotions are designed to foster goodwill between a company or government and its present or potential customers."[17]

An example would be an oil company promoting the positive uses of energy for society rather than ads for its gasoline stations. The objective could be to combat negative press they have received from an oil spill.

---

[17] businessdictionary.com

Churning Out Crap

"There really is no such thing as a boring subject. Just boring, unimaginative writers" —Ben Hurt

Ask yourself if you would spend your own money to run the ad you just created for your client.

When I started in advertising back in the day and there wasn't a lot of work, the agency would have the creative people produce generic ads. The agency placed them in a file and when an unsophisticated client (sucker) came along, they would just stick his name and logo on the ad and present it with a dog and pony show. The client thought we created it just for him.

I worked for a small agency in Huntington, Long Island and each week we created multiple generic car-dealer newspaper ads, complete with a rough drawing of a car racing down the street. We ran them off on the photocopier and we customized three ads for each dealer in the area. We presented the same ads to every dealership in town, but with their name on the top. The dealer, who said 'yes' first, got the ad. We would use different generic ads for the next dealer as we marched down Northern Boulevard cold calling. Each dealer thought we created a special ad, just for them. Since they were basic and non-specific it was easy to customize the dealers ads with their name and catchy headline.

If Jack Sprat Dealership (See illustrations on next page) chose Ad 1, we'd eliminate that design for Joe Blow and Phil Sims and so forth down the line. With so many dealerships in Nassau and Suffolk Counties, it required a dozen or so different layouts and some footwork to nail down a few dealerships. But once we had the accounts, we had repeat business each week. If we lost an account, which was common, we'd just repeat the process.

Often we'd call on the same dealership with new layouts and headlines for months before landing the account. One manager said, "You boys must really care about my business. You're in here every week with fresh new ideas. Let's try a few out." He had no idea he was just one in a long string of prospects seeing the same sample ads.

The same practice can be used today even though newspaper readership is at historic lows. There are plenty of opportunities in radio, social media and web advertising.

Jack Sprat Dealership	Joe Blow Dealership	**Phil Sims Dealership**
March Madness Blowout	**March Madness Blowout**	**March Madness Blowout**
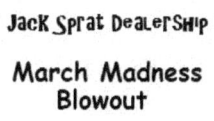		
kjdoid ijLjlaij jdljdla ljsl jsljkslkj kdalsjlkj kjdlajljlakj lkjljlkjlkjlkj lkhjsjlkj lkj lkjljljlkj	kjdoid ijLjlaij jdljdla ljsl jsljkslkj kdalsjlkj kjdlajljlakj lkjljlkjlkjlkj lkhjsjlkj lkj lkjljljlki	kjdoid ijLjlaij jdljdla ljsl jsljkslkj kdalsjlkj kjdlajljlakj lkjljlkjlkjlkj lkhjsjlkj lkj lkjljljlki

Jack Sprat Dealership	Joe Blow Dealership	**Phil Sims Dealership**
Come on Down For Savings	Come on down for Savings	**Come on Down for Savings**

kjdoid ijLjlaij jdljdla ljsl jsljkslkj kdalsjlkj kjdlajljlakj lkjljlkjlkjlkj lkhjsjlkj lkj lkjljljlkj	kjdoid ijLjlaij jdljdla ljsl jsljkslkj kdalsjlkj kjdlajljlakj lkjljlkjlkjlkj lkhjsjlkj lkj lkjljljlki	kjdoid ijLjlaij jdljdla ljsl jsljkslkj kdalsjlkj kjdlajljlakj lkjljlkjlkjlkj lkhjsjlkj lkj lkjljljlki

Jack Sprat Dealership	Joe Blow Dealership	**Phil Sims Dealership**
$1 over Invoice	**$1 OVER INVOICE**	$1 Over Invoice

kjdoid ijLjlaij jdljdla ljsl jsljkslkj kdalsjlkj kjdlajljlakj lkjljlkjlkjlkj lkhjsjlkj lkj lkjljljlkj	kjdoid ijLjlaij jdljdla ljsl jsljkslkj kdalsjlkj kjdlajljlakj lkjljlkjlkjlkj lkhjsjlkj lkj lkjljljlki	kjdoid ijLjlaij jdljdla ljsl jsljkslkj kdalsjlkj kjdlajljlakj lkjljlkjlkjlkj lkhjsjlkj lkj lkjljljlki

The following week we repeated the process with a new series of generic ads. The agency's philosophy was that the dealers were too afraid not to advertise in the newspaper and it cost them nothing extra since the paper paid us a 10% commission and our production costs were low. If a full page ad cost the client $3,000, our commission would be $300 less about $25 in production costs. That left about $275 profit on each ad. By selling six ads a week, the agency generated $7,000 a month.

In 1974 dollars that was great income for a two man agency with one employee. We had other accounts as well. They demanded and received good quality work. The dealerships ads was like picking low hanging fruit every week. No real effort involved.

The way to write good advertising is to make it specifically for a client's product or service. In the above example, we should have studied a particular dealership, the way they run their business, their pricing, service and customer relations. From this, we would spend several days to develop a unique concept for a campaign, work up fresh ad dummies and then present it to the dealership. This type of speculative work is labor intensive and expensive for the agency, but it's the right way to do it.

I discussed this with the agency owner who just laughed, "Mike, I used to work that way and it almost cost me my business. I picked up the technique from another 'ad man' who was retiring. The bottom line is that it works. The dealerships buy them, and I can in turn meet your paycheck each week. In all honesty, I don't see a big difference from one dealer to the next. I'm not going to change as long as it works."

The sales technique worked well for this small agency, but how did the ads work for the dealership? Did they really increase sales? It was impossible to determine. The dealers were too afraid not to advertise and ran something every week, so there was no benchmark to measure the ad's effectiveness.

How then, do you write good advertising? I learned a great technique in the SVA class "How to Write an Ad and How to Make it Better" to determine if an ad is good or bad. First read the ad out loud. Second, re-read the ad and substitute the competitor's name for the sponsor's name. If the ad still makes sense and is a true statement, then it is a bad ad. Why? If you can substitute the brands that easily, then the consumers, in their rush, will certainly do so. They may remember the ad but not the product name. How many dramatic or funny ads can you think of and have forgotten the product's brand name? I have seen ads that were so broad and generic that they could be used by the competition and by products in entirely different industries.

Often a soft drink company will run ads with the objective to motivate consumers to buy a buy a cola, any cola. Their expectation is that the ad will generate a large volume of sales in the entire category of beverages and that they will get some of that volume in proportion to their market share. This form of generic advertising is an expensive and inefficient way to sell. They do it only because the manufacturers can spend millions running the campaigns and repetition makes an impact.

Try this test. Take a weekly magazine and flip open to a soft drink ad. (A print publication is easier to use for this exercise than the internet.) Find another ad from a competing soft drink, cut out the photo of the product and the logo then place them on top of the first ad to cover the original soft drink and logo. Now read the ad substituting the name of second product for the first one. If the ad had appeared that way originally, would you have known the difference?

Both manufacturers want to sell you their brand of soft drink, but may have nothing unique to say about their product. Their respective agencies create an image of a guy and girl with windblown hair, sitting on a blanket at the beach. The ad suggests, to a male reader, that if he wants to get the beautiful girl, he needs to buy her a soft drink.

The same philosophy applies to generic car ads. An ad entices you to shop for a new car -- any car. Each manufacturer hopes you choose theirs, of course. If the entire marketplace (a pie) sells 1,000 cars a week and a manufacturer has a 20 percent market share, he will sell 200 cars. If his ad can increase the total volume (make the pie bigger) to 1,100 cars a week, then he will sell 220 cars. This represents his 20 percent market share. If, at the same time, he can increase his market share to 21 percent with a USP, he will then sell 231 cars.

Most creative people know when they are producing bad advertising. It's not, however, always in their power to decide which campaign runs. Instead, the client makes the final decision. The agency may produce two or three different ad campaigns for a product, then show them all to the client to choose. Frequently the client will pick the worst ad, because they are not trained in the creative and persuasive process.

The agency tries to do good work, but in the end it's the client who pays the bills and the one they must please. It seems ironic that a company will hire creative people, spend millions on an advertising campaign, then tell the agency how to do its job. These same people would never think of telling their family doctor how to practice medicine. On the other hand, maybe they would.

Examples:

I've created a headline and copy for a pick-up truck campaign. I will insert different brands as the sponsor. Note how that they are interchangeable and therefore bad.

Chevy Silverado

Headline: More Power, More Cargo Room, Better Ride

Visual: Photo of truck parked at a job site with a man working behind it.

Copy: The new Chevy Silverado Truck was built with you in mind. We've increased the horsepower, stiffened the suspension for heavier payload and increased the cargo area. But we didn't forget that you have to drive it, so we've given it a smoother quieter ride.

Come see the new Chevy Silverado at your local Chevy dealer.

Tagline: Chevy Trucks, like no other.

Insert logo

You've seen that type of ad a million times, even if you're not in the market for a truck. And to a novice copywriter it might seem like a good ad, professional done. But let's take that same ad and see if it's generic enough for the competition.

Ford F-150

Headline: More Power, More Cargo Room, Better Ride

Visual: Photo of truck parked in an open field, with two ranch hands loading bales of hay.

Copy: The new Ford F-150 Truck was built with you in mind. We've increased the horsepower, stiffened the suspension for heavier payload and increased the cargo area. But we didn't forget that you have to drive it, so we've given it a smoother quieter ride.

Come see the new Ford Truck at your local Ford dealer.

Tagline: Ford Trucks, like no other.

Insert logo

And now, let's see how it works for Chrysler.

Dodge Ram

Headline: More Power, More Cargo Room, Better Ride

Visual: Photo of truck parked in an open field, with two ranch hands loading bales of hay.

Copy: The new Dodge Ram Truck was built with you in mind. We've increased the horsepower, stiffened the suspension for heavier payload and increased the cargo area. But we didn't forget that you have to drive it, so we've given it a smoother quieter ride.

Come see the new Dodge Truck at your local Dodge dealer.

Tagline: Dodge Trucks, like no other.

Insert logo

These are fictitious ads for real products. If you had seen any of those ads, would you have been able to link the headline and copy to a particular truck? The ad is generic enough that anyone could use it, including Toyota, Nissan and others.

Let's look at an ad I created that uses a USP. The verbiage is modified from Motor Trend's and Ford's websites.

Headline: Ford F-150, Motor Trend's 2012 Truck of the Year

Subhead: Motor Trend Editor-in-Chief Edward Loh announced the Ford F-150 as the 2012 Motor Trend Truck of the Year at a Ford press conference.

Visual: The F-150 in a dramatic setting

Body copy: In a Head to Head comparison, the Ford F-150 received the coveted Motor Trend's Truck of the year award for our outstanding quality, performance and value. The F-150 is a tool built for a purpose. It has a goal in life and its heritage goes back to 1948. Go online and see the F-150 put through its paces in grueling punishments and stop by your local Ford dealer for a test drive.

Tagline: Built Ford Tough Insert Logo [18]

Ford had a USP that no other truck manufacturer could make, even if Chevy and Dodge made a case that their 2012 trucks were superior, only Ford could run a campaign as Motor Trend's truck of the year for 2012. It would be false and misleading for anyone else to make that claim. And that title stands till they rate the 2013 model. If Dodge or Chevy win next year, it will be their turn to brag.

The question begs, is this USP strong enough to increase sales volume. Year-end sales results as benchmarked against prior year sales will determine that outcome. It also depends how much Ford promotes the USP.

---

[18] Source: www.motortrend.com and www.ford.com

This exercise demonstrates the difference between a generic concept and a USP. You should always look for a USP in your client's product or service. Sometimes it's dramatic, sometimes it's minor and sometimes you can find the USP buried in in the copy on their website or in their catalogue.

Assignment:

Following are actual ad headlines. Write down as many other categories the exact headline could be used in and still make sense. How many do you think were the first idea that popped into the head of the person who wrote them? How product specific are the headlines that you write?

"The Future Begins with You" – online vocational school

"A Better Way to Find the Best Deal" – search engine

"A Smarter Choice" – medical clinic

"We Make Customer Service Our Priority" – car dealership

"We're Here for You" – real estate agency

And my favorite generic headline, "You've Tried the Rest Now Try the Best" – local Brooklyn pizzeria. And they do make great pies.

It's Not as Easy as it Looks

"It may well be that creativity is the last unfair advantage we're legally allowed to take over our competitors." —William Bernbach

Advertising is like sales; everyone thinks they can do it.

I was working at an agency when a client presented us with a sketch drawn by his eight-year-old daughter. It was a cute drawing and deserved a prominent place on the refrigerator. He wanted us to use it in the campaign. We did our best to discourage him without insulting his daughter's work, but he insisted.

Would this client let his eight-year-old come to work and balance his books, or give him legal advice on a patent infringement suit? Would he let her reprogram his computer? Of course not; however, she was allowed to develop the concept and create the artwork for a million dollar advertising campaign that could determine the success or failure of the company.

We lost the account when the campaign failed to drive business up. The client switched to another local agency and their new campaign still had the child as a spokesperson. She spoke in a high pitched, rapid voice that we understood only because she used almost the exact same script; the script the client wrote and insisted that we use. The only script changes were a few that we had recommended but the client had initially rejected. Think of her performance as a 30 word run on sentence, but she looked cute in her Shirley Temple curls.

I believe 75 percent of the advertising you see is bad. This has caused companies with good products to generate poor sales results.

Me Too Products

"Poor copy cannot overcome faults or gaps in dealer distribution; it cannot even cash in on the finest dealer setups. But good copy can, and does, surmount many dealer difficulties, making them secondary, and selling in spite of them."
Victor Schwab

A "me too" product is a copycat of another product, said another way, it is a product that is identical to other products on the market.

Examples are hairpins, book matches, thumbtacks and sugarless gum. There is no question of quality and they all do the same thing as their competitors.

"What do you do if there is no USP? Invent one." --Jay Wolf

Assume your client makes window glass cleaner. It's identical to every other glass cleaner on the market. You take the basic ingredient ammonium hydroxide, that every cleaner contains, and give it a special name: Clapp-a-San. Then you register it as a trademark. You can now advertise your product as: "The only glass cleaner with Clapp-a-San." Does that sound familiar?

Another method is to eliminate an ingredient and make that your USP. One national brand removed alcohol from its ingredients and created a new line extension as the only alcohol free window cleaner.

The feature was the elimination of harsh chemicals. The benefits listed were safe for delicate surfaces, tinted glass and painted kitchen cabinets, auto windshields, mirrors, navigating displays, Plasma TV screens, clear plastic acrylic windows, convertible top plastic windows, boat and RV windows. That USP held until other brands followed suit. Their new USP became, "The Original Alcohol Free Window Cleaner."

You may sell the identical product for the same price as everyone else, if so, make the USP the quality of service provided.

All of the service stations in a small town sell name brand gas at the same price. They all sell gas and oil, most have a convenience store attached and have an air hose for your tires. To differentiate himself from the other "me too" stations, one owner offers to vacuum the customers' car or a free car wash with each fill up. He has now set himself apart from the pack and the others must play catch-up to maintain their market share. As a consumer, with all else being the same, which station would you choose?

Look closely at the product and service and what the competition offers. How can you make your client's brand stand out?

A company makes a toothpaste that is a cash cow; a product that generates profit with little or no investment of advertising or marketing. In layman's terms it's a product that sells itself.

Unfortunately, this cash cow had a minuscule market share and was difficult to keep on the shelves at major chain stores. These chains would not stock any product that had a market share below a certain percentage. The company created a new classification, "Adult Toothpaste." The product became the number one adult toothpaste by default since it was the only toothpaste in that category. Their market share went from near zero to 100 percent. No retailer wanted to be without the number one adult toothpaste. They succeeded in stabilizing their cash cow.

Tink of the Energy bar revolution. A candy bar reformulated and sold in a brand new category that didn't exist twenty years ago. Now self-respecting adults can indulge in a treat without guilt.

Unique packaging can be the USP such as single serve portions, biodegradable material and less plastic wrap only if they are the only one who offers it. It can transform a "Me Too Product" overnight.

Features vs. Benefits

"If you say something about your product and the customer says, SO WHAT,
it's a feature. If he says, WOW, then it's a benefit."
John Glenn, Sales Manager Procter & Gamble

A feature is an aspect of your client's product or service. An example is that they sell an on-line investment software program that allows investors to buy and sell stocks. One of the many features is a "Customized Daily News Update." (SO WHAT?) The benefit is what that feature will do for the investors. The News Update sends them an e-mail or text on any stock splits, earnings reports and mergers. They can customize it for any stock, mutual fund and news item they prefer. This gives them valuable information that occurred overnight that would affect their investment before the market opens. (WOW!)

Here is a scenario demonstrating the difference between the two.

Bill is a brand manager trying to explain his company's new ballpoint pen to Joe, the agency copywriter. Bill is talking about features; however, the copywriter is listening for benefits. See if you can tell when Bill stops talking "SO WHAT" and starts talking "WOW."

"Joe, unlike any other disposable pen, our ball point pen has a pressurized ink cartridge."

"So what?" Joe asked.

"The ink is kept under constant pressure." Bill says.

"So what?"

"The ink flows at a constant rate."

"So what?"

Bill wondered why the copywriter didn't get it. The benefit is perfectly clear. Bill gets technical. "The air pressure in the cartridge forces the ink toward the ball point at all times."

"So what?"

"NASA developed the pen for use in space travel."

"So what? Next time I fly into space, I'll buy one."

Bill thought to himself, this copywriter is dumb as a brick; any idiot can see the benefit. I better spell it out for him. "The benefit is that the pen will write at any angle, even upside down. So when you're making notes on a clipboard hanging on the wall, or lying on your back while entering an inspection number to the bottom of a machine, the pen will always write, even in zero gravity. You don't have to stop every few seconds and shake the pen to make it work. It will even write on greasy paper."

"Wow! Now that's a USP. Why didn't you say so before?"

"I thought I did." Bill said.

Just because the benefit is obvious to you,

doesn't mean it's obvious to everyone else.

When self-winding watches were introduced about sixty years ago, the feature was self-evident to everyone. As long as you wore it, the movement of your arm kept the watch wound. Perhaps the mechanics weren't widely understood but you knew you no longer had to wind the watch every day to keep it running.

In the 1970s when the quartz watch was introduced, the benefit of a battery operated watch wasn't obvious. People believed it to be a variation of a successful product that was more accurate; since that was the way the company advertised it.

The benefit was that the watch would continue to run even if you took it off and left it on the dresser for a year. That was something a self-winding watch couldn't do. The ads only stressed the accuracy. The benefit wasn't self-evident to the public.

Long after the quartz watch was introduced, I met a guy at a communications class who wound his quartz watch every morning in the classroom.

"Why are you winding a battery operated watch?" I asked.

"I didn't know it had a battery. Aren't you supposed to wind it every day?"

"Nope. It's like an electric clock."

"I've wound it every day for the last year. It works fine," he said.

"All you're doing is spinning a watch stem that isn't attached to anything except the gears that adjust the hands. It has no mainspring. There is nothing to wind. Let me show you," I said.

I flipped the watch over and pointed to the battery cover, unscrewed it, removed the battery and showed him his watch had stopped. I replaced the battery and the watch worked again. He then understood the benefit of a quartz watch.

"Oh. Now I feel stupid. I had one last year that stopped working no matter how much I wound it. I thought it was broken, tossed it and bought a new one."

"When you bought the watch, did the sales clerk tell you how it worked?"

"I don't think so."

"Was there anything on the display case that told you about the battery and the benefits?"

"Not that I remember."

"No need to feel stupid. It's that no one explained how the watch works. Now when it stops, take it to a jeweler and get a new battery installed," I said.

When you write copy, talk about the benefits to the customer. If you mention features, make sure it is linked to a benefit.

Examples of a feature linked to the benefit:

Feature: A shampoo and conditioner in one. (So What)

Benefit: Easier and faster to use since you only have to buy a separate conditioner. Saves money. (WOW)

Feature: Digital camera with video (So What)

Benefit: All in one. You no longer have to have to carry two devices. (WOW)

Feature: Remote key fob (So What)

Benefit: You no longer have to pull a key out of your pocket or purse to open or start the car. (WOW)

Once you master the Feature vs Benefit, you can add another step, the Advantage. It is the link between the Feature and Benefit that helps make the connection clear to the consumer.

FEATURE: Our GPS uses a 4G internet connection.

ADVANTAGE: You can access the map quicker than with 3G

BENEFIT: You can swiftly find your way to your destination.

How to discover the benefits

1.) List every feature of your product or service.

2.) Determine the need for each feature.

3.) Think of how each feature can connect with the consumer.

4.) Determine what's in it for the consumer emotionally.

5.) Prioritize the features from most important to least.

6.) Select the one that is a USP. (if any)

7.) If there is no UPS, make the strongest Feature-Benefit the concept for the ad. Don't forget to include the Advantage.

"Consumers do not buy products. They buy product benefits." – David Ogilvy

Assignment:

Below is a list of features for Electric-Vehicles (EVs). Turn the SO WHAT Features into WOW Benefits and include the Advantage for each.[19]

1.) All-Electric vehicles run only on electricity.

2.) They are propelled by one or more electric motors.

---

[19] https://www.fueleconomy.gov/feg/evtech.shtml

3.) They are powered by rechargeable battery packs.

4.) EVs have several advantages over vehicles with internal combustion engines.

5.) Energy efficient. EVs convert about 59%–62% of the electrical energy from the grid to power at the wheels—conventional gasoline vehicles only convert about 17%–21% of the energy stored in gasoline to power at the wheels.

6.) EVs emit no pollutants, although the power plant producing the electricity may. Electricity from nuclear, hydro, solar, or wind-powered plants causes no air pollutants.

7.) Performance features. EVs provide quiet, smooth operation and stronger acceleration and require less maintenance than Internal Combustion Engines.

Parts of a Traditional Print Ad

It is far easier to write 10 passably effective sonnets than
one effective advertisement.

–Aldous Huxley

HEADLINE the attention grabber

VISUAL photo of the product or event

BODYCOPY the details

LOGO company branding

TAGLINE usually a short term campaign line, sometimes a

company motto.

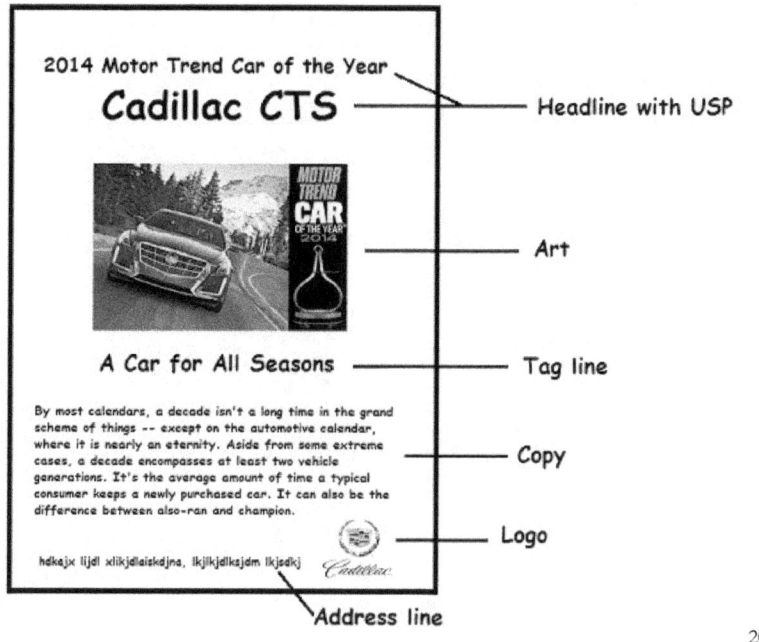

Using the information on the MotorTrend website, I found all the information for this sample ad. The body copy is for illustration purposes only.

Assignment:

Visit the MotorTrend website listed in the footnote and write 80 words of copy from the supplied editorial. Use the Features and Benefits provided to create a call to action.

---

[20] http://www.motortrend.com/news/2014-motor-trend-car-of-the-year-cadillac-cts/

The Steps of Creating an Ad

"Make it simple. Make it memorable. Make it inviting to look at.
Make it fun to read." – Leo Burnett

There are no hard and fast rules in the business. To coin a phrase I just made up, it's more art than science, but don't discount science.

There is no guarantees that if you follow my advice step by step that you will always create a great ad, but by eliminating many of the amateur mistakes, you can stand head and shoulders above the crowd. And remember that no matter how great your campaign is, if it is a lousy product or priced wrong, it will be a flop.

Developing a concept

The concept of any advertising the framework in which you build the campaign. It must be simple, direct, uncluttered and calls the consumer to action. This is a fancy way of saying your ad is dynamic enough to get the consumer to drop whatever he or she is doing, hop in their car, drive to the mall, find your product and buy it and it's no easy feat. As an example, the cell phone competition is fierce, yet customers lined up for days at the Apple store to be the first with the new iPhone.

I have an iPhone but I waited a year before I bought my first one. I wasn't that motivated. I did; however, see a commercial about a new drill bit that could remove screws with stripped heads. I was restoring an old piece of furniture and the screw slots where the phillips head screwdriver fit was rounded out on a half dozen screws. My only options were to dig into the wood enough to get a vice grip on the head and back it out or use a metal drill bit and try and bore the old screw out without damaging the wood too much. It was frustrating and I had set the task aside until I thought of a resolution. A month later I was watching a cable show and they had an infomercial about the a new drill bit that could remove stripped screw heads without damaging the wood. I sprang from the couch, drove to the big-box hardware store and bought one. I didn't even look at the price, I just snapped it up. When I returned home, I immediately tried the bit and it worked just as advertised. Now that's a call to action.

The added burden of everyone in Advertising, is working for clients who fancy themselves as creative people and try to tell us how to do our job. We had great designers who produced contemporary, visually appealing layouts only to have the client over-rule them with amateurish, confusing and poorly designed layouts. Since the client

pays the bills, they usually win the debate. Welcome to Advertising.

When developing a concept, step one is to study as much as you

can about the product. Look at their current advertising, read the

user manual, look online for product information and reviews by

outside sources. Study the competition as well to see what others in

the industry are doing. You don't want to copy them but rather get a

feel of the industry trends.

Make a list of the things you think are important. A soft drink or

candy campaign would be different from a pharmaceutical or

electronics campaign.

For a candy bar, you want to focus on the enjoyment and

satisfaction of a craving, a reward for hard work or just simple

pleasure. Highlight the ingredients to appeal to consumers who like

those things. Snickers has a "You're not you when you're hungry"

campaign. Cranky actors morphed into ordinary people when their

hunger is satisfied. (This is not a USP since other snack foods could

have done the same campaign successfully.) We are talking candy

bars. That doesn't mean a candy bar ads can't have a USP but usually

they don't. If you do find a USP is it significant and worthy of attention? Keep in mind the balance between the USP and its value. Will the value resonate with the consumer?

Once you have a list, take a note pad and write down every idea that comes in your head no matter how stupid or brilliant they may sound. Then, take the list and put it in a drawer for seven days. After you have let the ideas percolate in your brain for a week, take the list out and read it. You will see just how lame the ideas are. Throw the paper in the trash to symbolically erase them from your head and write a new list. This will be the list that contains a gem of an idea for your campaign. Trust me on this. Most of the bad advertising you see is the result of some account executive or brand manager using the first thing that pops in their mind.

T-Mobile has a campaign using a USP. T-Mobile, Largest 4G Network and this is a strong USP because 4G is cutting edge and is, as of this writing, the largest 4G network. Note they don't claim to be the only 4G, but the largest. If Verizon or AT&T builds out their 4G to be the largest, then T-Mobile will have to stop making that USP claim.

Let's study the USP potential of some of the examples:

Volkswagen: Surrounded by safety

Can Volvo, Mercedes and Ford make the claim that they build safe cars? If so, then "Surrounded by safety" is not a USP. That doesn't mean it's a bad campaign. They want to project the image of their cars being safe to drive. The official VW website lists at least 11 safety features of their car. To hammer the point home, it is a strong campaign but not a USP unless you can make the case that the VW is the only car with theses 11 safety features.

Coca Cola: Believe in a Happier Tomorrow

What do you say about a soft drink? Is this a campaign to drive the brand or drive the soft drink market? Who else could use the same campaign?

Pepsi Cola: Believe in a Happier Tomorrow

Dr. Pepper: Believe in a Happier Tomorrow

7 Up: Believe in a Happier Tomorrow

Do they all make sense? Would you know the difference if another product had run the ad?

There is no doubt Coke campaigns are successful. I can remember one of the Coke jingles from my childhood. The 1960

Coca-Cola Ad - "Only Coca Cola Gives You That Refreshing New Feeling" sung by Anita Bryant and the Brothers Four. That was 52 years ago. You can find the spot on YouTube.

Ford Mustang: They don't make cars like they used to. We do.

I'm a big Mustang fan and I've owned two, a 1965 and a 2005. Without a doubt, the 2005 is superior to the original, mechanically, in performance, durability, fit and finish. With this perspective, having first-hand knowledge how cars were built in the 60s, I would not say this is the way to go with a campaign.

My suggestion, not that the folks at Ford will listen to me, is to say, "We took a great idea and made it better" and show the 1964 and 2016 side by side. The body copy would compare the two in all categories including horsepower, engine displacement, dash cluster and so forth. Rather than battle the new Camaro or Dodge Charger for the retro market segment, they compare their new model to their own iconic car. This is a gray area for the USP. The VW Beetle, Camaro and Charger could do the same campaign since they are all higher quality than the originals. However, it would have mass appeal to the Mustang fan base.

Do you want caffeine or decaf with that headache? Tylenol

This is a nice play on the caffeine free aspect of the product. When Tylenol was introduced, their USP was Tylenol, the only aspirin free pain reliever. Today's campaign is not a USP but well done visually and reinforces the caffeine-free feature.

Determine if the following campaigns utilized a USP. Rate their effectiveness.

About the only think it can't help you with is writer's block. -- Apple Mac Powerbook circa 1993

Sony Cyber Shot camera: Super Clear with Super Zoom

Assignment:

Find a current campaign that uses a USP and one that does not. With practice, you will be able to tell is an ad is a dud or a winner.

Writing a Headline

"On the average, five times as many people read the headlines as read the body copy. It follows that unless your headline sells your product, you have wasted 90 percent of your money."

David Ogilvy

There are exceptions, but most ads have a headline composing 8 to 10 words.

Even though this is a copywriting book I need to make a design point. Using all caps in headlines containing more than four words is a real bad idea. All caps is difficult to read because fonts were designed to be written in upper and lower case. It is how we are trained to read. In addition, all caps on the internet symbolizes shouting and is rude. We have all been victims of someone's email or blog where they write 10 paragraphs in all caps. I usually quit reading it after the first sentence. Initial caps are fine. Now that I have that off my chest, back to writing headlines.

A headline is the attention grabber that stops the reader from turning the page, tossing the direct mail piece or clicking on the next link on your webpage. A headline needs to scream at the reader: STOP and read me.

The headline and the visual, (if there is one) should contradict each other, they should never deliver the same message.

An example:

Enjoy a Sliced Orange

The orange has more vitamins, minerals and fiber than an apple. And the additional energy it provides is balanced by the added nutrient benefits. Include both fruits in your diet, but if choosing just one, the orange is a healthier selection. [19]

Orange Growers of Florida

In this fictitious ad, the visual repeats the headline. The body copy explains the benefits of the fruit but will readers make it past the headline and visual to get that information? It's not a compelling ad and a complete waste of advertising dollars.[22]

---

[21] Photography by Mike Swedenberg
[22] Which is Healthier, an Apple or an Orange? Livestrong.com By Tara Carson

Now consider this conflicting headline and visual:

Guess What Really Keeps the Doctor Away

The orange has more vitamins, minerals and fiber than an apple. And the additional energy it provides is balanced by the added nutrient benefits. Include both fruits in your diet, but if choosing just one, the orange is a healthier selection. [1]

Orange Growers of Florida

"The sole purpose of the first sentence in an advertisement is to get you to read the second sentence." – Joseph Sugarman

---

23 Photography by Mike Swedenberg

You have creative license and are excused from most spelling and grammatical rules within reason. An ad for a dyslexia support service could read:

Headline: READING SI ERUTROT

Body copy: You and I see it as Reading is Torture but many with

Dyslexia see half the sentence backwards.

In this example, misspelled words are acceptable. But I saw a newspaper ad some years ago that read: "Your going to love our new menu."

How many editors did this get past? And using your instead of you're is not a typo, it's a grammatical error. Unless your concept uses a misspelled word or bad grammar intentionally, it is not acceptable.

Urban legend: "Never use a negative or the word 'no" in a headline." I have heard this so called rule since day one but like everything else it has its place. Refer to the classic Volkswagen ads from the 1960s:

Lemon.

This Volkswagen missed the boat.

The chrome strip on the glove compartment is blemished and must be replaced. Chances are you wouldn't have noticed it; Inspector Kurt Kroner did.

There are 3,389 men at our Wolfsburg factory with only one job: to inspect Volkswagens at each stage of production. (3000 Volkswagens are produced daily; there are more inspectors than cars.)

Every shock absorber is tested (spot checking won't do), every windshield is scanned. VWs have been rejected for surface scratches barely visible to the eye.

Final inspection is really something! VW inspectors run each car off the line onto the Funktionsprüfstand (car test stand), tote up 189 check points, gun ahead to the automatic brake stand, and say "no" to one VW out of fifty.

This preoccupation with detail means the VW lasts longer and requires less maintenance, by and large, than other cars. (It also means a used VW depreciates less than any other car.)

We pluck the lemons; you get the plums.

24

Why is this VW a lemon? The chrome strip on the glove box

was dented. The car was pulled off the line and repaired.

They broke the rule and made Madison Avenue history.

=

24 Created by Bill Bernbach - BBD ad agency,

Some Grammar Ruled do Apply

Active voice is preferred over passive. "You win the race" is better than "The race was won." Avoid boring verbs; stride is better than walk. Check this excellent blog for a complete list of boring verbs with special thanks to Clay Held[25]:

> A weak headline is an open invitation for everyone
> to ignore your ad.

Weak Headline:

New Policy at County Line Dealership

Boring, nothing interesting here folks.

Keep flipping the pages.

Strong Headline:

County Line Chevrolet, Buy One Get One Free

When you buy any new 2012 Chevrolet and bring it to us for an oil change, you'll receive a free oil change on your next visit no matter how long you have owned it, the make, where you bought it or even if you inherited it from your dear Aunt Mildred.

---

[25] http://www.clayheld.com/2010/07/22/50-boring-verbs/

Be direct and brief. The fewer words in your headline are better as long as it communicates the message.

Assignment:

Go through a magazine or print ad and find a long-winded headline. See how many words you can delete without destroying the message.

Additional reading with special thanks to Lawrence Bernstein[26]:

[26] http://www.infomarketingblog.com/100-good-advertising-headlines-victor-schwab/

Subheads

"Nobody reads ads. People read what interests them. Sometimes it's an ad." –
Howard Gossage

A Subhead is an additional message following your attention grabbing headline. It gives the reader more information, features and benefits to encourage them to read the rest of your brilliance. They should tell their own story. Here are a few examples I created:

<u>Headline: New Pain Relief Treatment</u>

Subhead: Academy Pain Management offers a new FDA approved treatment for chronic back pain accepted by most insurance policies.

<u>Headline: The Vegan Diet Made Simple</u>

Subhead: Written by three top chefs and two nutritionists and featured in Health Magazines.

<u>Headline: Making Money the Old Fashioned way – on eBay</u>

Subhead: A step by step guide. How the other sites like Amazon differ. Creating your own store, what to sell, what to avoid, the scams that can wipe you out, all for $9.95

Writing Body Copy

"A copywriter should have an understanding of people, an insight into them, a sympathy toward them." – George Gribbin

This is the meat and potatoes of an ad. Regardless if it's in print, TV, brochure, flyer or electronics, it contains the details of your concept. This is your last chance to motivate the reader into action.

There are five steps to making a face to face presentation. It is an effective tool developed by Procter & Gamble. No matter what you sell, a product or service, no matter what the media you should follow these steps as written. Don't switch them around, don't eliminate any of them. Since you are selling through a print ad, TV spot or electronically you get one chance. You cannot probe, ask questions, discover and overcome objections.

Here are the steps:

1. Summarize the Situation

2. State Your Idea

3. Explain How it Works

4. Reinforce Key Benefits

5. Suggest an Easy Next Step.

1.) Summarize the Situation. First, get the readers' attention.
Your first line of copy should be as dramatic as the headline.
Say something to peak their interest enough to make them
continue reading and devote a few minutes to what you have
to say. Let's use the headline I created for a fictitious ad and
product as an example.

Headline: New Pain Relief Treatment

Subhead: Academy Pain Management offers a new FDA
approved treatment for chronic back pain accepted by most
insurance policies.

Visual: Man holding his back as if in extreme pain.

BODYCOPY

Attention grabbing first sentence: "No relief for your chronic
back pain?"

It addresses those who suffer from chronic back pain or knows
someone who does. Grammatically, it is a fragment, an incomplete
sentence. You can envision your High School English teacher
reaching for her red pen to circle your mistake, but it doesn't matter
here. We need to be brief. If you suffered from back pain like the guy
in the visual, would you keep reading or would you say "Ho hum,"

and flip the page?

2.) State your Idea and say what you want the reader to do: "Academy Pain Management has an answer. We invite you or your loved one who suffers from chronic muscular pain to visit our facilities for a free no obligation consultation." Is there any confusion in your mind what the ad is asking and offering?

3.) Explain How it Works: Detail exactly how the program works. Anticipate the objections the reader may have and address as many of them as possible. "The FDA has just approved a radically new and effective treatment for chronic muscular pain. It involves no surgery or medication. The Radial Sonic Blastanator has proven effective in marked relief or total elimination of pain in as little as three treatments."

4.) Reinforce Key Benefits of your offer. Emphasize what is in it for the reader. <u>Emphasize the benefits not features</u>: "You now have an alternative to surgery and pain medication. Our treatment is FDA approved and covered by most insurance. You have nothing to lose except the pain."

5.) Suggest an easy Next Step or Trial Close: A close is when you ask for the business. This is a trial close because you are not sitting face to face with the reader. You need a call to action. You don't need to beat the reader over the head. Make a soft close: "If you are someone you care about suffers from chronic pain, stop in for a free no obligation examination and consultation. A board certified pain management specialist will answer all of your questions. Call 555-595-4000 to arrange an appointment."

Insert Academy logo, tag line and address, web address. The tag line will be discussed in the next section.

Now, you have to make the copy quick and snappy. The body copy has 135 words. That is too long. Eliminate unnecessary words. No one wants to read your dribble.

Here is the body copy without the editorial comments:

No relief for your chronic back pain? Academy Pain Management has an answer. We invite you or your loved one who suffers from chronic muscular pain to visit our facilities for a free no obligation consultation. The FDA has just approved a radically new and effective treatment for chronic muscular pain. It involves no surgery or medication. The Radial Sonic Blastanator has proven effective in marked relief or total elimination of pain in as little as three treatments. You now have an alternative to surgery and pain medication. Our treatment is FDA approved and covered by most insurance. You have nothing to lose except the pain. It involves no surgery or medication. The Radial Sonic Blastanator has proven effective in marked relief or total elimination of pain in as little as three treatments. If you are someone you care about suffers from chronic pain, stop in for a free no obligation examination and consultation. A board certified pain management specialist will answer all of your questions. Call 555-595-4000 to arrange an appointment.

Keep the copy to about 80 words. A technique I use is to mentally charge myself $25 for each word over 80. Said another way, I wrote 172 words in my draft. 172 words minus the allowed 80 words equals 92 times $25 each equals $2,300. That is a fine I have to pay myself for having diarrhea of the mouth. No way am I paying that much. I have to edit the copy and decide what changes I can make to get the count down to 80 and still maintain the integrity of the message. If I cull it down to 81, will that extra word be worth $25?

For the sake of clarity, I will list the body copy by sentence to show the edits I made. I have to eliminate 72 words. I must be brutal.

No relief for your chronic back pain? (This is perfect. No changes.)

Academy Pain Management has an answer.

We invite you or your loved one who suffers from chronic muscular pain to visit our facilities for a free no obligation consultation. (I'm combining these two into one sentence.)

Revised: Academy Pain Management invites everyone with chronic muscular pain to visit our facilities for a free consultation. (This eliminates 12 words.)

The FDA has just approved a radically new and effective treatment for chronic muscular pain.

It involves no surgery or medication. (Again, I combine two sentences)

Revised: The FDA approved a radical and effective treatment for chronic muscular pain. No surgery or medication. (I saved 5 words.)

The Radial Sonic Blastanator has proven effective in marked

relief or total elimination of pain in as little as three treatments. (This has 21 words)

Revised: The Radial Sonic Blastanator, proven effective in pain relief or elimination in as little as three treatments. (Now 17 words, a savings of 5)

You now have an alternative to surgery and pain medication. (10 words)

Revised: An alternative to surgery and medication. (6 words)

Our treatment is FDA approved and covered by most insurance. (10 words)

Revised: FDA approved and covered by most insurance. (7 words)

You have nothing to lose except the pain. (8 words)

Revised: I eliminated this sentence. It's a cliché and unnecessary. (8 words saved)

If you are someone you care about suffers from chronic pain, stop in for a free no obligation examination and consultation. (21 words)

Revised: Suffer from chronic pain? Get a free no obligation examination and consultation. (12 words)

A board certified pain management specialist will answer all of your questions. Call 555-595-4000 to arrange an appointment. (18 words)

Revised: A board certified pain management specialist is available. Call for an appointment. (12 words. The phone number is in the address line, but you may leave it in the copy if you wish without penalty.)

The first revision has 100 words. Better but still 20 words over budget.

No relief for your chronic back pain?

Academy Pain Management has an answer.

Academy Pain Management invites everyone with chronic muscular pain to visit our facilities for a free consultation.

The FDA approved a radical and effective treatment for chronic muscular pain, no surgery or medication.

The Radial Sonic Blastanator, proven effective in pain relief or elimination in as little as three treatments.

An alternative to surgery and medication.

FDA approved and covered by most insurance.

Suffer from chronic pain? Get a free no obligation examination and consultation.

A board certified pain management specialist is available. Call for an appointment.

Let's see what else we can cut without hurting the message.

Academy Pain Management is mentioned twice in the copy. That is overkill. It's already in the Subhead, first line of copy and in the logo.

Academy Pain Management has an answer.

Have chronic muscular pain? Visit our facilities for a free consultation. (I'm eliminating this. "We invite everyone with..." is too wordy. Gone.)

An FDA approved treatment for chronic muscular pain with no surgery or medication.

The Radial Sonic Blastanator, proven effective in pain relief or elimination in as little as three treatments with no surgery or medication. (Combined two sentences into one.)

Covered by most insurance. (Eliminate FDA approved. Already stated that.)

Suffer from chronic pain? Get a free no obligation examination and consultation.

A board certified pain management specialist is available. Call for an appointment.

Draft three is down to 80 words. But how does it read?

Academy Pain Management has an answer.

Have chronic muscular pain? Visit our facilities for a free consultation. An FDA approved treatment for chronic muscular pain with no surgery or medication.

The Radial Sonic Blastanator, proven effective in pain relief or elimination in as little as three treatments with no surgery or medication.   Covered by most insurance. Suffer from chronic pain? Get a free no obligation examination and consultation. (This line is redundant. I'd rather use the words to say something else.)

A board certified pain management specialist is available. Call for an appointment.

After more editing, draft four of the body copy is 61 words long. Remember the headline, subhead, FDA mandatory copy and address line does not count in the 80 word limit.

Reading is clear and concise with 104 fewer words. Can you spot the changes? I now have the option to add 19 words or leave it as is.

How would you modify it? Here is the complete ad ready for layout and design:

=

New Pain Relief Treatment

Academy Pain Management offers a new FDA approved
treatment for chronic back pain accepted by
most insurance policies.

Academy Pain Management has the answer if you suffer from chronic muscular pain, visit our office for a free consultation about a treatment without surgery or medication.

The Radial Sonic Blastanator, proven effective in pain relief or total elimination in as little as three treatments is here. Don't suffer.

Our board certified pain management specialists are available. Call for an appointment.

Logo, address line and tag line.

Taglines

"The consumer isn't a moron; she is your wife. You insult her intelligence if you assume that a mere slogan and a few vapid adjectives will persuade her to buy anything." – David Ogilvy

A tagline is a message that is associated with your company and usually follows the company logo. Some companies change their taglines frequently to reflect changing products or trends like the many taglines of Coca Cola including "Can't Beat the Real Thing" "Coke Is It" "Have a Coke and a Smile" "Catch the Wave"

Others get one and run with it forever. Like 'A Diamond is Forever"- De Beers "Just Do It - Nike, "got Milk?" - California Milk Processor Board. American Express has three: "Do more," "My life. My Card," and the iconic "Don't leave home without it."

Other famous taglines are

Finger-lickin' good -KFC

Taste the Rainbow - Skittles

Nobody better lay a finger on my Butterfinger! - Butterfinger

Eat fresh –Subway

Examples:

Volkswagen: Surrounded by safety

Coca Cola: Believe in a Happier Tomorrow

Ford Mustang: They don't make cars like they used to. We do

Do you want caffeine or decaf with that headache? Tylenol

About the only thing it can't help you with is writer's block.

Apple Mac Powerbook circa 1993

Sony Cyber Shot camera: Super Clear with Super Zoom

Snickers: You're not you when you're hungry with Betty White and other actors.

T-Mobile: Largest 4G Network

Taglines are short and often times memorial slogans associated with a brand. As you can see by the examples above most are three to four words long, a few like Butterfinger are seven words long. Firestone tires tag line from the 1960s and 70s "Where the rubber meets the road," still lives inside my head. I can't recall any others, not even Michelin. I'd have to Google them to find out.

More though and meetings take place when a company chooses a tagline than for a short lived ad campaign. Some contain USPs and others are generic.

A recent debate raged on a LinkedIn discussion blog about the best taglines. One poster said BMWs "The Ultimate Driving Machine" was the best in his opinion as a professional copywriter. However, when I challenged him to justify his selection, he became defensive. BMW spent a ton of money promoting their brand and tagline, but my point was that any high-end car company could have used the slogan, "The Ultimate Driving Machine." Who is to say that Mercedes, Lincoln or Porsche wouldn't have adopted that line if BMW didn't take it first?"

I asked my fellow copywriter if he honestly though that Mercedes Benz would have turned down that tagline because they didn't think they were worthy? "Oh no, Mr. Copywriter. Only BMW deserves to be called the Ultimate Driving Machine, not our humble $183,000 Mercedes, SLS AMG Gullwing grocery grabber." I never heard back from the copywriter.

My point is that when you are creating a tagline for your client; keep in mind their advertising budget and the USP principle. Do they have the money and years BMW has to promote their brand identity? And what is the Mercedes's tagline? Beats me, I'd have to look it up. In a way The Ultimate Driving Machine is a good tagline, but is it worth the cost? How is it different from the hundreds of Pizzerias in

New York who claim "You've tried the rest now try the best." Do smaller companies have the budget to brand their products the same way? Has it sold any BMWs?

And there you have it. An overview of the art of copywriting. For you kids in your twenties, pick up that funny looking bundle of papers that comes out every day. It's called a newspaper. You see old geezers like me reading them. Flip through the pages and look for the different size ads. Study them, read them and break them down into components. This is cutting edge work and someone is paying a lot of money to produce and publish them. If you find one that's good, set it aside for future reference. If you find one that is bad, and this will be easy to do, fix it.

I have a friend, who started his ad agency who did this to find new clients. He found bad ads in the newspaper for local merchants and rewrote them. He made a pitch to the retailer presenting his idea in exchange for the paper's 10% commission plus any special production charges like photography. And it worked.

Another friend, Sam Chinkes built his agency years ago by cold call canvassing for new business. I asked Sam how he did it.

"I had self-confidence in my ability to understand any prospects' needs and in my ability to produce the art and copy to satisfy them. I chose an industrial area and just 'knocked on doors' regardless of the type of business there.

In three hours, I called on ten firms and came home with three checks, down payments on one trade publication ad and two small brochures. Total up front: $400.00."

-Sam Chinkes samchinkes.com

Does it work all of the time? No.
Does it work most of the time? No.
Does it work some of the time? Yes.

With constant effort you can build a portfolio of clients. There is nothing stopping you. And if you don't have the computer skills to create the artwork, find someone who does and partner up with him or her. Or, go to a small agency and say you'll help them bring in new accounts if you can do the copywriting. Don't forget to get a percent of the fees and put it all in writing.

Now get off your butt and start writing ads that sell products.

ABOUT THE AUTHOR

Mike Swedenberg, a native of Greenville South Carolina, moved to New York to attend the School of Visual Arts where he studied Concept, Copywriting and Design. He later worked in sales and marketing and spent 30 years in corporate America.

Mike graduated from Adelphi University on Long Island with a business degree. He studied creative writing at the Gotham School of Writing in Manhattan and fine art painting at the Long Island Academy of Fine Art. He teaches How to Publish an eBook at Nassau Community College and has authored a dozen books.

Sam Chinkes
Sound Advertising, Las Vegas

Other books by the Author

A New York Wedding – a novel
Bully Boss – a novel
The Road Warrior a sales manual
Advertising Copywriting and the Unique Selling Proposition
Study Guide to the US Citizenship Test (in 8 languages)
The Short Stories of Mike Swedenberg

Index

www.ingramcontent.com/pod-product-compliance
Lightning Source LLC
Chambersburg PA
CBHW070830180526
45168CB00002B/788